5 MINUTE HISTORY

ANDREW ROBERTSHAW

FIRST WORLD WAR
TRENCHES

First published 2014

The History Press
The Mill, Brimscombe Port
Stroud, Gloucestershire, GL5 2QG
www.thehistorypress.co.uk

British Library Cataloguing in Publication Data.
A catalogue record for this book is available from the British Library.

ISBN 978 0 7509 5452 5

Typesetting and origination by The History Press
Printed in Europe

CONTENTS

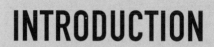

INTRODUCTION

MANY PEOPLE IMAGINE that the war started on the Western Front in 1914 and ended in 1918, was fought entirely in trenches and that there was little movement or open warfare over the more than four years of the struggle. This book aims to explain how trench warfare came about, to put this style of conflict in a historical perspective and to explore what caused the deadlock on the Western Front. It will examine the routine of trench warfare, the experiences of men on both sides of no-man's-land and how the trench stalemate began in 1914 and ended during 1918.

In films and on television the First World War is portrayed as being about the battles. The Somme in 1916 or Passchendaele in 1917 are presented as being typical experiences for the soldiers on the Western Front. In these on-screen presentations, trenches are places from which attacks over no-man's-land are launched or repulsed with bloody casualties. Soldiers do not live in trenches, they only die, and the day-to-day experience of being in a hole in the ground is defined by shelling, gas, constant rain and, perhaps, war poetry. I want to use this *Five Minute History* to explain the details of life in the trenches in addition to exploring the day-to-day reality of the men who took part in the war on the Western Front.

Since 1985, first at the National Army Museum in London and then in other museums, schools, colleges and universities, I have taught up to half a million young, and not so young, people about the First World War. I have used my illustrated presentation 'Eye Deep in Hell?' – note the question mark – with hundreds if not thousands of groups. Responses to this talk have ranged from questioning to outright disbelief. Some people believe that what they see on the screen in *All Quiet on the Western Front* or *Blackadder Goes Forth* are adequate representations of history and that anything else is clearly 'wrong'. One veteran of the First World War described his experience of the trenches as being '90% bored stiff, 9% frozen stiff and 1% scared stiff'. Another suggested that his war was experienced 'in colour', not the black and white of the photographs and original film we see today. If this book succeeds, I want the reader to have an understanding of the 99 per cent of trench warfare the men experienced on an everyday basis and to bring some colour into the sepia world of 1914–18.

ASR,
Spring 2014

WAS TRENCH WARFARE NEW IN 1914?

BY OCTOBER 1914, as we will see, warfare on the Western Front, from the Swiss border in the south to the coast of the North Sea in Belgium, was locked into static trench warfare. Both sides had dug in either side of a strip of land, which became known as no-man's-land. No one could move in this area in daylight and both sides worked in the night, when darkness allowed men to dig and erect barbed wire. However, this was not the first time soldiers had worked under similar conditions.

In previous centuries, when an army was dispatched to surround and besiege a castle or town, the use of cannon or siege engines on both sides meant that the attackers had to protect themselves from enemy fire. The defenders had the advantage of earth or stone defences which had been designed and built as a permanent protection, whereas their opponents had to provide themselves with some means of cover while being close enough to the place they were besieging to use their artillery. The result of this was that besiegers would surround their objective and then start to dig in at night, when their opponents would have difficulty seeing and shooting at them.

I WAS THERE

I was on a working party the other day down at the trenches, and I took one of the Minie rifles and went to the front and I picked off three men at about eight hundred yards.

Lieutenant Vaughan, in the siege lines at Sevastopol, 1854[1]

DID YOU KNOW?

A private soldier in the modern Royal Engineers is called a 'sapper', in historical reference to the work of these soldiers in digging 'saps'.

This work was planned and started by engineers – the technical service responsible for constructing defences. The engineers were responsible for digging the siege lines or *zaps*, as the Italians called them. These curving trenches – 'saps' to the British – were dug into the ground and the excavated material was thrown up or packed into bags or woven baskets of sticks called 'gabions'. The siege lines of saps surrounded the place under siege and were gradually extended forward towards its defences. Night was always the safest time to work, but both sides used artillery or individual marksmen with accurate muskets, like today's snipers, to pick off the unwary enemy soldier. A soldier from the First World War transported back in time to a siege of the time of the Duke of Marlborough or even Napoleon would have been familiar with the layout of the trenches that made up the siege works. The big difference between his trenches and those of earlier periods was their extent – not across an entire country, only around a city or castle – and for the duration of the fighting. This was normally measured in weeks or months, as the defenders had limited resources of food and unless help came they would either face starvation or the horrors of an all out assault by the attackers.

Advances in weapons technology meant that the techniques of siege warfare were increasingly used on the battlefield. By the American Civil War, 1861–65, individual soldiers could hit targets at 1,000 yards. This compared to 100 yards a generation earlier. One result was that both sides took to digging pits for protection if a battle became a stalemate. Between June 1864 and March 1865, the Confederate defenders of St Petersburg in Virginia found themselves facing a 'modern' version of siege warfare, which went on for nearly ten months. The Union attackers used mining at one point and exploded a gunpowder charge under enemy lines in the expectation of breaching their defences. This attack was unsuccessful but represented a small-scale representation of the Western Front fifty years later.

I WAS THERE

At Modder River there was no human interest – just a bare plain and 800 yards off, a line of trees; not a Boer, or even a puff of smoke to be seen all day; only, if one raised his head, the ping of a bullet and the sight of another dead or wounded comrade.

Sir H.E. Colville, the Battle of the Modder River in the Boer War[2]

DID YOU KNOW?

In 1865, Union forces succeeded in blowing up a mine filled with gunpowder under the Confederate trenches at St Petersburg in Virginia. The attack that followed was a disaster.

The armies of Europe rejected the lessons of the vast citizen armies of the American Civil War and, although there were sieges in the Franco-Prussian War, 1870–71, nothing resembling trench stalemate reoccurred until the Second Boer War in South Africa, 1899–1902. Here barbed wire, which had been invented in 1874, was combined with automatic weapons and this resulted in some brief periods of trench conflict. Trenches were used by the Boers defending positions such as Colenso, and when surrounded by the British at Paardeberg the following year, the Boers dug in for a brief period before being forced to surrender. Isolated British garrisons held out during Boer sieges at Mafeking and Ladysmith behind wire defences and trenches, but these were isolated incidents in a war of movement.

However, in 1904, when Russia went to war with Japan, the attack on the Russian-held town of Port Arthur provided an example of how modern weapons, tactics and defences might influence future warfare. Although only a siege, the Japanese attacks used artillery and mortars against Russian defences which featured true machine guns, barbed wire and searchlights combined with the use of shovels and pickaxes to dig saps that gradually moved closer to the defender's positions. The decider in this conflict was the mass use of Japanese artillery and the Russian defences were eventually breached, ending a five-month siege. This siege was a miniature version of the future Western Front in which the outstanding feature was the heavy loss of life on both sides.

Lessons from this costly war were not lost on the armies of the world and books on the use of machine guns, barbed wire and artillery were produced and read by military experts. All of whom were aware that another, bigger war was possible if the armies of Europe were

DID YOU KNOW?

Russian prisoners from the war of 1905 were well treated by their Japanese captors. They set up a brewery and bakeries in the Japanese city of Kobe that continued in production after the Russian 'guests' were returned home at the end of the war.

put in motion by events that would lead to mobilisation of the millions of men under arms in the vast conscript armies of both sides in the Triple Alliance of Germany, Austro-Hungary and Italy, and the Triple Entente of France, Russia and Great Britain.

THE 'EUROPEAN WAR' 1914

WHEN EVENTS IN Sarajevo in June 1914 triggered the road to war, which broke out in August that year, virtually no one predicted a long struggle and even fewer foresaw trench warfare being a possibility. With the exception of Great Britain's British Expeditionary Force, which was equipped for a highly mobile campaign of open warfare, the armies of Europe had prepared for siege warfare, but only as one element in the conflict. They were aware that the fortresses which littered the main routes of advance would need to be captured and that the arsenals of both sides featured heavy siege guns, mortars and even flare guns and signal rockets. If attacks on the forts occurred, which appeared inevitable, the siege and defence would last days or weeks, and it was planned that the campaign would be over in a matter of months. Some people predicted that it 'Would all be over by Christmas' and the German Kaiser suggested a more optimistic 'All over before the leaves fall from the trees'; what would occur if this did not happen was not considered.

I WAS THERE

The French cavalry is animated by a thoroughly patriotic spirit. All officers understand and subscribe to their doctrine and theory, which is clear and simple, both in tactic and training.

Report on Foreign Manoeuvres in 1912[5]

DID YOU KNOW?

Some historians believe that the Schlieffen Plan was drawn up to demonstrate that the German Army was too small for the task and only a much larger force would be successful.

For the Imperial German Army a triumphant campaign that would take them to Paris in a matter of weeks was confidently predicted. They were aware that the Russians would mobilise in the east, but thought it would be a slow process. The objective as laid down in the Schlieffen Plan was to aim a rapid knockout blow at France, capturing Paris within six weeks. This attack would be aimed at the weak spot of the French defences by coming through neutral Belgium, bypassing the main French defences. It would then move like a vast opening door pivoting on the Swiss border in the south and engulfing Paris from the north-west. This rapid victory would allow the bulk of the German forces to then be diverted east to protect Prussia and avoid a war on two fronts.

The French people had been left bitter by the defeat in the Franco-Prussian War of 1870–71. They were anxious to avenge the loss of two French provinces, Alsace and Lorraine, which were annexed by Germany in that war. Many French commentators predicted that an attack to recapture these lost areas would lead to a war of movement. A French attack on Germany aided by the mobilisation of the vast Russian 'steamroller' that would invade Germany from the east could, it was believed, lead to the fall of Berlin and victory.

Only a few voices urged caution and suggested that the war could become protracted. The British Chief of the Imperial General Staff, Field Marshal Kitchener, echoed the Polish banker and war theorist Bloch, who thought that the war might last years. Lord Kitchener suggested in 1914 that the decisive year would be 1917. British war aims were to ensure Belgian neutrality, as agreed by a treaty in 1837, and to co-operate with the French, as agreed in the pre-war *Entente Cordiale*.

DID YOU KNOW?

The German Schlieffen Plan aimed to avoid a war on two fronts with both France and Russia. The intention was to destroy the French Army and capture Paris before sending German forces east to defeat the Russians.

DID YOU KNOW?

The French Army of 1914 went to war in red trousers and blue greatcoats as a means of appealing to the spirit of the Emperor Napoleon and his revolutionary army of a century before.

The tiny, all-volunteer British Expeditionary Force would supplement the millions mobilised by France in resisting the German assault, while, as dictated by Lord Kitchener, a New Army of volunteers was to be raised and trained to join in the struggle. When the first shots were fired in August 1914, what few predicted was that within months both sides would be sitting in trenches on the Western Front.

OPENING MOVES
IN 1914

IN MANY WAYS, the opening campaigns on the Western Front in the late summer and autumn of 1914 were very similar to those of Napoleon 100 years earlier. Although initial mobilisation was speeded up by the use of railway networks, once the German armies crossed the Belgian and French borders the advances happened at the speed of marching men and horses. Mechanised warfare was in the future and it was boots and hooves, not tracks and tyres, that were typical of 1914. Importantly for the story of trench warfare, although there were sieges of defended cities and fortresses such as Liege and Namur, the war did not become one of trenches. Instead, the vast armies, numbering millions, advanced or retreated over hundreds of miles in a style of warfare that Napoleon or the Duke of Wellington could have understood. Machine guns could slow attackers, but not stop them, and the advantage of magazine-fed rifles with long ranges to defenders also

DID YOU KNOW?

The first and last British soldiers to die in the First World War are buried in the same cemetery as each other at St Symophorien near Mons in Belgium.

I WAS THERE

I searched through my glasses. Yes, there among the buildings away at the end of the meadow was a faint haze of smoke. Then in God's name let us get closer. 'Forward again – at the double!' We crossed the track, then jumped the broad dyke full of stagnant water on the far side and then across the squelching meadow. Tack, tack, tack, tack! – srr – srr – huitt – tschui – tshui – tschui! – cries – more lads falling. 'Down! Open fire – far end of meadow – range 1000 yards!' And so we went on, gradually working forward by rushes ...At every rush a few more fell, but there was nothing we could do for them.

Captain Walter Bloem, 12th Brandenburg
Grenadiers, at Mons, August 1914

favoured attackers. There was little barbed wire, other than that placed by farmers, and cavalry was able to carry out reconnaissance and even mount charges in this phase of open warfare. Casualties were heavy, as was the use of ammunition, but the ability of countries to stockpile and manufacture munitions, combined with their ability to mobilise a large percentage of their manpower, meant that losses could be replaced.

By early September 1914, German forces were in sight of Paris and their victory appeared certain. The British Army had fought well at Mons, in Belgium, on 23 August, but had been forced to retreat into France to keep contact with the French, whose weak left flank was pushed back, and avoid the Germans getting between the Allied forces. French plans in the south had not gone well and little ground had been gained from the Germans. The retreat from Mons took the British Expeditionary Force back down the roads towards Paris, and the French made a similar retirement on their front. By the time the armies reached the River Marne, the last major obstacle to the German advance, a repeat of the Franco-Prussian War and defeat appeared inevitable. What followed was described at the time by the French as 'the miracle of the Marne'.

DID YOU KNOW?

It was a pilot of the Royal Flying Corps that spotted the German Army's change of direction in September 1914, which indicated that they would not outflank Paris.

With its force's back to the city and with the final river defence about to be breached, the German advance slowed and then halted. Although French commanders were convinced that it was their forces that had pulled off the victory, it was distance, exhaustion and shortage of German soldiers that meant their advance had finally ended within sight of the Eiffel Tower. The German Army had relied upon their speed of advance to overcome the defenders and had anticipated that a rapid victory would mean their supplies of ammunition, rations and fodder for the horses would be sufficient for a brief campaign. The hot weather of August combined with the distance advanced took a toll on the men and horses. Rations became so short that whole units were told to halt so that their transport could be used elsewhere.

I WAS THERE

We dug those trenches simply for fighting; they were breast-high with the front parapet at ground level and in each bay we stood shoulder to shoulder.

Private Frank Richards, at Ypres, November 1914[5]

Worse still, by the time they reached Paris it was clear that there simply were not enough German soldiers to confront the French Army and British Expeditionary Force without gaps appearing in their lines. German High Command had no choice other than to move men further south, shortening the front of the army and putting Paris out of reach.

However, the period of open warfare was not over. Although units had dug small scrapes in the ground with their entrenching tools at various points to provide temporary cover, there were no lines of trenches. Nevertheless, the Germans were aware that victory was still possible. Although they and their opponents were in contact and in combat in places from Paris to the south, the situation to the north was quite different.

Here units of the hard-pressed Belgian Army and French forces were resisting the German advance. There were wide gaps between the troops and both sides, and the Germans could exploit this situation if they could get fresh troops into the gap between the forces near Paris and the North Sea. What followed is referred to as the 'Race to the Sea', but was in fact an attempt to turn the flank of the opposing army. If this could be achieved, one force would find that enemy troops were behind them, and if one force could get behind the other troops they would be outflanked and cut off from supplies. This did not happen as both sides poured troops into the gap and the line of trenches extended further north until they ended on the North Sea coast. With victory in their grasp, the German High Command decided to pull back and to dig in on the most tactically advantageous positions possible. This would allow them to hold on to as much occupied ground as possible, while reducing the number of men required to hold the line. Men in trenches, combined with well-suited artillery, machine guns and barbed wire, could hold a greater frontage than men in the open. While this process was going on, troops could be spared to move into the gap between the increasingly well-defined line of trenches in the south and the sea.

DID YOU KNOW?

The French believe that one of the deciding factors in the 'Miracle of the Marne' was the military governor of Paris General Gallieni's idea to send reserve forces across the river in taxis.

I WAS THERE

Numbers of German dead lay close to our trenches. An officer of the 4th D.G.'s was asked why he didn't clear away one corpse that could be reached by bayonet from the trench. 'Oh, Sir,' the officer replied naively, 'he is quite inoffensive.'

Frederick Coleman, chauffeur attached to Sir John French's headquarters, Ypres, November 1914[6]

STALEMATE

BOTH ARMIES RUSHED troops north and the line of trenches extended as the forces met and fought themselves to a standstill. On the Somme, later to become infamous in 1916, the German troops arrived in early October 1914. At Ypres, the last city in Belgium still in Allied hands, the German Army and British Expeditionary Force, who had been sent to this sector as a deliberate policy to demonstrate support for Belgium, fought a battle in November. This First Battle of Ypres resulted in the creation of a salient around the city with the Germans on the high ground and the British, French and Belgians on the low ground facing them. This area would claim over 400,000 casualties over the four years of the war and the city would be shelled flat in a series of major battles.

By late November, open warfare was over and both sides had entrenched from Switzerland and the North Sea. Options for manoeuvre were over and trench stalemate had been created. However, both sides looked for ways in which this deadlock could be broken and a victory achieved.

For the Germans the trench statement could be seen as the logical solution to their failure to win the war in the west as they had planned. By digging in, they could afford to send troops east to deal with the Russian threat while

DID YOU KNOW?

The French Army had lost half a million men killed, wounded and captured by Christmas 1914 and a million by the same time in 1915.

holding on to the ground they had occupied in the opening months of the war. If they could achieve conclusive victory against Russia they could end their war on two fronts, and then put all their troops to face the Allies in the west to achieve final victory.

The situation for the Allies was more complex. They could not win the war by staying where they were. The trenches were built in French and Belgian soil and millions of men, women and children were now in occupied territory, behind the lines. The industry, agriculture and economy of these regions were being used by the Germans to support their war effort and there were indications that the enemy did not intend to give the occupied territory back. The Allies would either have to fight for it or negotiate with the occupiers and agree some form of peace terms. The Allied politicians decided that the armies of France, Belgium and Britain would hold the existing trench lines while looking for ways in which to push the enemy back and end the trench stalemate.

I WAS THERE

During the whole of Boxing Day we never fired a shot, and they the same, each side seemed to be waiting for the other to set the ball a rolling. One of their men shouted across in English and inquired how we enjoyed the beer. We shouted back and told him it was very weak but we were very grateful for it. We were conversing off and on during the whole day.

Private Frank Richards, Christmas 1914[7]

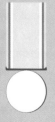

DID YOU KNOW?

The famous Christmas truce of 1914 was largely between British and German troops rather than those of France or Belgium because the British and Germans were not on land that meant anything to them.

The result of this was that for most of the war, until Russia was forced to surrender in late 1917, the Allies attacked and the Germans defended on the Western Front. The only major exception was the Battle of Verdun, launched by the Germans in February 1916. This attack on the French fortress city of Verdun was intended 'to bleed France white' by killing so many of her troops that the French Government would have to ask for peace terms from Germany.

One method of ending the deadlock on the Western Front without achieving the breakthrough both sides sought was to be victorious in other theatres of operation. Whilst the Germans and their Austro-Hungarian allies sought to achieve victory in the east against the Russian Army, Italy joined the war on the side of the Allies. Turkey, too, was drawn into the war and an Anglo-French force attempted to invade the Turkish homeland in a landing in Gallipoli peninsular in early 1915. This operation

I WAS THERE

The German trenches are 150 to 250 yards distant. His shell fire is trivial, but the least exposure draws a sniper's bullet, and infinite care is necessary when examining his lines through binoculars. For this purpose one wears a brown woolly cap instead of our too-conspicuous black Glengarry bonnet, and the head must be raised ever so slowly into the niche in the sandbags on the top level of the trench.

Brigadier General Jack, at Houplines, France'

became bogged down in trench warfare and was abandoned in early 1916. Despite an expedition to Bulgaria and landing in Salonika, by 1916 it was clear that the only way to end the war on the Western Front was a conflict of attrition that would lead to the collapse of the Germans or the Allies.

Trench warfare on the scale of the First World War had not occurred before 1914, simply because armies were too small and weapons ineffective to allow a war to happen on a front that spanned national boundaries. Mass conscript armies based on increased populations meant that there were sufficient men and weapons to hold a front not of a few miles, but of 450 miles. Importantly, these new weapons worked well in trench conditions, whereas black powder muskets and cannon would not, and new methods of preserving food meant that it was possible to feed millions of men even in winter.

DID YOU KNOW?

The British Expeditionary Force arrived on the Continent without the loss of a single ship or man because the Royal Navy was so powerful.

Until the twentieth century, armies were forced to go into 'winter quarters' for the coldest months of the year to ensure that the men and horses could be fed and housed. This did not happen between 1914 and 1918.

DID YOU KNOW?

When German reserves arrived by train at the old border with Belgium in October 1914, the signs had already been changed to read 'Welcome to New Germany'.

DIGGING IN

THE FIRST TRENCHES were simple scrapes in the earth, sometimes behind cover such as a hedge or as an improvement to an existing ditch. The tools used to do this were variations of 'entrenching tools' carried by combatant soldiers. These tools were small and easily carried as part of a soldier's equipment. They were adequate for a soldier who was lying down on a battlefield to excavate a hole; the earth was thrown in front as additional cover and concealment. Some soldiers, such as the Germans, used their packs as additional cover and as rifle rests while doing so.

Once the war of movement was over and deeper trenches were necessary, the tools and nature of the work changed. Full-size picks and shovels were brought forward to the front line, and the men worked at night, as they had to stand to use these tools. As infantrymen were not trained in siting trenches, the engineers usually selected the location of the trenches and laid them out using white tape and pegs so the men could see where to dig. Locations such as the tops of hills, where men's heads would be exposed on the skyline, or positions susceptible to enemy fire along the trenches were carefully avoided. However, with little experience of this type of warfare, many men would be lost to errors and bad planning. When digging trenches, the men usually worked so that some were on or in front of the position ready to shoot, while others took it in turns to dig, pickaxe and, when available, fill sandbags. Shortage of these essential items meant that many early German trenches were built with looted pillowcases.

Trenches depended on their design to provide the best possible protection to the users, as well as on the nature of the soil in which they were dug. The front-line fire trenches were designed with fire bays – an area slightly in front of the main position provided with a fire step on which a soldier could stand to use his weapon. These bays were subdivided into sections a few feet long so that a shell bursting a bay would kill or injure the minimum number of defenders. This subdivision also meant that, should an opponent get into the trench, he could not fire along the line of it.

DID YOU KNOW?

The term 'parapet' for the front of a trench and 'parados' for the back are derived from the French *para tete*, meaning cover the head, and *para dos*, cover the back.

I WAS THERE

The breastworks are some 7 feet high, 7 feet wide at the top and 18 at the bottom. About 6 feet behind the front wall there is a similar wall, with a trench 2 foot deep between the two. The inner face of both walls is revetted with sandbags, and solid traverses every ten yards protect the men in the bays from enfilade fire as well as localising shell bursts ... On the enemy's side of the parapet a wide ditch, boggy in wet weather, and a thick belt of barbed wire serve to prevent surprise attack.

Brigadier General Jack, 1915

The dividing blocks were called 'traverses' and were not used for shooting, as a firer may well hit his own men to the front. Instead, these areas were used for dugout entrances, when these were created, and were where the communication trenches linked to the front line.

Communication trenches were simply curving trenches along which the men could move below ground level. Supplies, reinforcements and casualties were all moved along these trenches, and some areas had a system of up and down trenches to avoid bottlenecks.

There was never just one line of trenches and different combinations of cover and fire trenches – first, second and third lines – were used in combination with reserve lines and rest areas. The complexity of the system depended on the labour and ingenuity of the garrison, the material available for construction and the geology.

Clay soil around Ypres in Belgium was easy to dig when damp, but the trenches were liable to collapse when wet and were very prone to flooding. In some areas command trenches were constructed, which were built up rather than dug down to avoid becoming waterlogged. On the Somme, underlying chalk drained well but was difficult to dig and the white scars created by trenches or mining were obvious targets for the enemy. In the mountainous sector south of Verdun, German and French trenches were dug from solid rock. These required little support and were dry and mud free. However, shells that struck these trenches created rock splinters, which made them more effective and caused more casualties. Nowhere on the Western Front were conditions ideal for men living a largely nocturnal lifestyle in holes in the ground.

An item that was in short supply in 1914 was barbed wire. This important means of creating obstacles became increasingly available, but one problem was erecting the stakes on which the wire was attached. These were initially wooden posts that had to be hammered into the ground. However, frozen or hard ground meant that heavy mallets had to be used and even when padded with sandbags the noise of this activity was distinctive and, potentially, deadly if the enemy was alert. Nevertheless, as both sides were often carrying out this essential construction activity very close to

---

DID YOU KNOW?

Germans call sandbags 'earth bags', which is a much more realistic term, given their usual contents.

their opponents, some groups of soldiers ignored each other so they could complete their task with the minimum of disturbance or casualties. Wiring and working parties had to be constantly alert for flares or rockets, and men were trained to remain motionless when these illuminated the area, as movement would give them away.

NAVIGATING
THE TRENCHES

EARLY TRENCH SYSTEMS were easy to find your way around in. There was a simple front line and a few communication trenches. As the system was developed and new lines added, this new complexity increased the problems for the troops using them. There were few landmarks in a trench and putting your head above the parapet was best avoided. The result was that trenches were named and these names inscribed on signboards, often with the addition of a map reference so that the precise location could be located. The names chosen usually reflected the unit: place names related to the unit or commanders' names. Others were humorous references to personality or comedy. On the Somme, for example, a trench in Thiepval Wood was Meerut Street when an Indian unit was stationed there. Later the same wood had a trench added called Elgin Avenue while the 51st Highland Division was in occupation. At some point a communication trench was named Creepy Street. The German strongpoint at Beaumont Hamel was named the

DID YOU KNOW?

The mines exploded at Messines in June 1917 were heard in London and rattled windows on the south coast of England.

Hawthorn Redoubt from the distinctive trees on the ridge. German and French forces used the same system, and the *Heidenkopf* at Serre, laid out in 1915, was named after Regiment Heiden that did much of the construction. Whilst the massive fire trench on the ridge above was called the *Bayen Graben*, the Bavarian Trench. Other features on the battlefields were given similar names and the distinctive double towers of the pitheads at Loos became Tower Bridge, the feature called the *Heidenkopf* by the Germans became the Quadrilateral on British maps, while many French-named places used the original name but with a distinctly English pronunciation: Auchonvillers became Ocean Villas, and Foncquevillers Funky Villas. What made the potential confusion for the Allies worse was that Loos, as pronounced by the British Expeditionary Force, was 'Los' in French and that Lens was 'Lons'.

As the war progressed, mapping improved and the early haphazard methods were replaced by scientific approaches and increased accuracy. As such, trench names, at least in British service, were rationalised. Military maps of the day used a combination of map squares which used letters and sub squares within this that were denoted by numbers. It was decided that all trenches within each letter square

I WAS THERE

Then we went the wrong way and had to turn back, nerve-racked and crowding each other ... At last the guide found the way again. He had come upon a surprising landmark – a group of dead bodies.

Lieutenant Ernst Junger, 73rd Honoverian Fusilier Regiment[10]

would be named with words that began with that letter. The consequence of this was that the author's grandfather, serving with the 12th Battalion, Manchester Regiment, was badly wounded in an attack on the German-held Wit and Wool trenches, on what was nominated Greenland Hill near Arras, in May 1917.

A complicating factor in mapping trenches was that they extended underground in addition to being on the surface. The first shallow and vulnerable dugouts were gradually replaced by a system of deeper shelters that were excavated by miners, and by 1917 they were capable of holding hundreds of men plus services such as headquarters, hospitals, kitchens and communications. These received names and numbers, which then had to be added to the increasingly complicated trench maps. To make this situation worse, saps and subways were used, especially in chalk areas, so that men could approach the front line in relative safety. These were a key feature of the Battle of Arras in 1917.

It is possible for battlefield visitors to undertake a guided tour of the Grange Subway at the Canadian National Memorial at Vimy Ridge by prior appointment. Linked to the 'passive' tunnels are a system of defensive and fighting tunnels that go far below the

DID YOU KNOW?

The crater at Beaumont Hamel replaced Hawthorn Redoubt in the explosion of 7.20 a.m. on 1 July 1916, which was filmed by the army cinematographer Geoffrey Malins. The same approach tunnel was used again for a second mine in the same place on 13 November 1916.

shallow system of subways and dugouts, and extend well out into, if not beyond, no-man's-land. These tunnels could be used to break into enemy tunnels or blow them in with underground explosions, killing the enemy tunnellers or entombing them alive in the wreckage of their galleries.

The most famous use of mines by the British is the attack on the Messines Ridge in June 1917. Here 21 miles were prepared but only 19 miles blown up in what proved to be a devastating and highly successful attack on the German-held position. Although some of the craters have been filled in, the most famous and easily visited near Ypres is Caterpillar Crater, close to Hill 60. The famous crater on the Somme is that of Lochnagar, started from the trench of that name near La Boisselle and blown on 1 July 1916. This crater is privately owned and one of the most well-visited spots on the Western Front.

A crater blown on the same day but now filled with trees is that of Hawthorn Crater, near Beaumont Hamel. Less well known and now filled in is Blue Pig Crater near Serre, where the war poet Wilfred Owen placed his machine guns when defending this sector in January 1917.

TRENCH WEAPONS

AT THE OUTBREAK of war, the weapons available to the men in the trenches were limited to rifles with bayonets and some machine guns. A few nations included grenades and flare guns in their stores in case of sieges. These were ideal for the trenches and all armies rapidly ordered flares and rockets to illuminate targets and signal for assistance. Grenades were excellent weapons for use in trench fighting or clearing dugouts and were soon in massive demand. In the British Army the first grenades were improvised and were made from empty jam tins filled with explosives and scrap iron, fitted with a fuse. To start with, this kind of device was as lethal to the users as the enemy and can be compared to the French bracelet bomb, which required the thrower to wear a band around his right wrist that hooked to the fuse on the ball-shaped bomb. When thrown, the bomb, in theory, was set fizzing on its way. However, if the hook and fuse did not separate, the thrower was still attached to his bomb.

DID YOU KNOW?

The British Army called grenades 'bombs' because the Grenadier Guards objected to anyone else using 'grenades'.

German troops favoured the use of stick grenades, which could be used in the open, as the fragments were small and did not travel far. A later development was to fit a device to a standard rifle that allowed the user to fire a grenade further and higher than by hand. Rifle grenades became a standard weapon in all armies and could be used alongside mortars in bombarding enemy trenches.

Like grenades, the first mortars were improvised weapons, and the French went so far as to reuse 300-year-old antiques because the principle of firing a fused bomb from one trench into another had not changed in that time. The Germans were able to develop a range of different-sized mortars very rapidly and they had a considerable advantage with these weapons for much of the war. Some British examples were borrowed from the French, but the simple mortar designed by Mr Stokes in 1915 proved to be the model for all future generations of this weapon.

Grenades, rifle grenades and mortars could be used to kill an opponent one could not see, but the big threat on all fronts in the hours of daylight was the sniper. Snipers used an accurate weapon fitted with telescopic sights and worked from concealed positions,

I WAS THERE

It was quiet just before zero and suddenly the sky was ablaze, as if lit by continuous flash-lightning. The thunderous roar of our artillery reached us on an instant as the screaming shells sped towards the target ... At zero plus fifteen minutes I opened fire and, with the aid of a shaded light and two pre-set pegs, kept the gun on its correct elevation and scope of traverse. I whipped through the first belt in less than half a minute.

Corporal George Coppard, Machine Gun Corps[11]

sometimes in the trenches, sometimes behind and occasionally from no-man's-land itself. There was never any warning of snipers and the man who looked over the top for too long or in the same place twice was likely to be hit. As the sniper took careful aim and the head was the most exposed part of the body in the trenches, sniper shots were frequently fatal. The result was that soldiers were always wary of standing too upright and aware of shallow trenches and damaged parapets. By mid-war snipers were used to observe and report on the enemy as opposed to simply shooting them, and their reports were used to inform intelligence units and the artillery.

From the outbreak of war, machine guns were an ideal weapon in trench warfare, but the water-cooled British Vickers or German Maxim were heavy and difficult to conceal. They also could not be easily carried forward into the attack or positioned to protect a vulnerable position in the front line. The result of this was that the British Army purchased examples of the Lewis automatic rifle, which was air cooled and relatively light, from the US company. By late 1915, the Lewis gun had entirely replaced the Vickers in the front line and these weapons were transferred to the new specialist Machine Gun Corps (MGC), which could use the long range of this weapon in force more effectively. The German response was to convert some of their Maxim machine guns to light weapons, although these retained the water jacket and were far heavier than the Lewis. Both French forces and the Americans used the French Chauchat as a light weapon, and the American-manufactured Browning automatic rifle entered service in 1918.

Raiding called for specialist weapons, as rifles with bayonets were long and cumbersome, and grenades noisy. If a silent attack was required, soldiers used trench clubs, which were like medieval maces, often made in workshops behind the lines. German troops favoured a standard entrenching tool with a sharpened blade, and these were reputed to be able to cut through a British helmet and the wearer's head. Some troops made use of pistols in raiding and men made some attacks with a pistol in each hand like a Western gun fighter. The actual combination of weapons and levels of concealment depended upon the nature of

DID YOU KNOW?
Of the six hundred and twenty-seven Victoria Crosses awarded in the First World War, fifty-five were for actions with pistols as the only weapon.

the raid and level of experience of the troops. The Germans had specialist raiding units, referred to by the British as the 'Bosch Flying Circus'. These expert raiders were able to use speed and stealth to capture prisoners, examples of new weapons and intelligence information. Cloudy, moonless nights kept all soldiers 'on their toes' and a poor sentry who failed to spot a raider wearing dark clothing had often made his last mistake. Both sides patrolled no-man's-land at night, even if there were no raids planned. Dominating this area was regarded as being vital to prevent men from becoming defensive and lacking in offensive spirit. Clashes in the dark were frequent, as the patrols clashed in the long grass and weeds between the lines and men were killed or wounded as they cut down this growth to clear 'fields of fire' and prevent the enemy using it as cover.

NEW WEAPONS OF TRENCH WARFARE

ONCE THE TRENCH lines had become established, both sides looked at new technology to break the stalemate. More machine guns, mortars or mining were useful, but they were not war-winning weapons. In the spring of 1915, at Ypres, which was always a focus for their attacks, the German Army used poison gas for the first time. The gas was chlorine, was stored in cylinders and delivered by means of pipes pushed out into no-man's-land. As the French and British defenders did not have gas masks – 'respirators' – it was uncertain how effective this first attack would be on the Allied lines. The gas had to be delivered with the wind in the right direction and, late in the afternoon of 22 April 1915, the gas was released. The gas was heavier than air and trenches soon filled with it, which when breathed in caused the sufferers' lungs to fill with fluid, drowning them on dry land. Despite great gallantry, a huge gap was torn in the trench lines north-east of Ypres. Canadian and British troops had great difficultly in halting the German advance, although this was finally achieved, but not without heavy casualties on both sides.

I WAS THERE

Gas shells were also coming over and we pulled our helmets [respirators] out ready to slip on as soon as we sniffed gas. There was no loud explosion with gas shells: they struck the ground with a soft thud and it was difficult to tell them from duds.

Private Frank Richards, 1918[42]

DID YOU KNOW?

The most famous victim of gas was Corporal Adolf Hitler, who was in hospital suffering from the effects of gas when the war ended on 11 November 1918.

Gas was no longer secret, and in September of the same year, British troops used gas against the German defences at Loos. By then all troops had a respirator and gas was developed by the scientists of both sides to overcome the various systems of barriers and filters being used. Chlorine was replaced with the much deadlier phosgene, and mixtures of gases were delivered by shell to overcome the vagaries of the wind. With the addition of mustard gas, which attacked human skin rather than the lungs or eyes, the arsenal of gas was virtually complete. Very few men actually died from gas, but many were to suffer its effects for years after the war. As a means of slowing down an opponent and causing him maximum problems, gas remained a potent threat until the end of the war.

Another weapon first used at Ypres was the flamethrower. Called the *flamenwefer* by the Germans, this was first used again at Ypres in May 1915. The attack at Hooge saw the use of a flamethrower that could be carried and operated by one man, and initially it was both terrifying and effective. However, the fuel was limited and the operator very vulnerable. Few flamethrower soldiers were ever captured alive. However, this did not prevent the British from developing their own weapons system that they referred to as a *flamenwefer*, and this was secretly demonstrated to the British Government inside White City football stadium, built for the Olympics in 1908. The comments of the groundkeeper were not recorded! A massive British flamethrower was used near La Boisselle in the attack on the Somme on 1 July 1916, and the Germans used a similar weapon in their defence in the same area. However, once again, the weapons proved to be only locally effective and were soon overrun or out of range.

What was needed was a weapons system that could get over the trenches, cut barbed wire and be protected from enemy fire while having its own offensive power. The British solution was the 'land ship', later given the code name of 'The Tank' to protect its real purpose. The original tank, named *Mother*, was based on an agricultural tractor and used tracks to get over soft ground. The hull was armoured and later two variations of weapons were used. The 'male' had two 6-pounder guns and the 'female' had machine guns. Although slow at 2½mph, it could cross trenches and no-man's-land and had impressive firepower.

Tanks were first used during the Battle of the Somme on 15 September 1916, at Flers, and were a complete surprise for the German defenders. Their effectiveness was limited by mechanical breakdowns and they were vulnerable to close-range rifle fire, grenades and, worse still, artillery. The wet Flanders clay limited their use at Ypres and the largest tank battle of 1917 was at Cambrai, in a bold attempt to capture this French town. Over 600 tanks were employed. Once again, however, mechanical problems, a stubborn defence and a German counter-attack limited their effect. On 8 August 1918, at the opening of what would become the '100 Days' advance that would lead to the Armistice, improved tanks were used in the

DID YOU KNOW?

The motto of the Tank Corps is 'Through the mud and the blood to the Green fields beyond', and they have a vertically striped brown, red and green flag.

highly successful Battle of Amiens. Although many tanks broke down, they were able to disrupt the German defences, and advances were carried out with tanks, armoured cars, infantry on lorries and even cavalry, which was much more similar to the open warfare of 1914. The British advance that followed Amiens was measured in hundreds of miles, not yards, although few tanks were in action after more than a few days. Tanks were not, yet, a war winner.

TRENCH LIFE

SOLDIERS IN THE trenches were seldom there for more than five days at a time once the early war shortages of men had been resolved by recruiting and a proper routine established. A unit usually took over a sector of trenches at night, going 'up' or 'into the line', guided into position by men from the outgoing garrison who could point out the location of dugouts, stores, vulnerable positions and threatening enemy weapons.

During the period when the unit was 'in the line', they were responsible for their sector, its defences and any improvements that had to be made. Units were judged on how well they maintained their sectors and the condition they were in when they left, and some were not careful with keeping the latrines clean, repairing damaged defences or generally tidying up. Trenches held by the Guards tended to be too tidy, with regular sandbag parapets, and this meant that their opponents could spot men peering over the top or the position of snipers quite easily. Trenches built or maintained by Bantam units, in which the soldiers could be as short as 5ft, would be death traps for taller soldiers, as they were often too shallow for them to move around in safety.

With enemy shellfire, sandbags that rotted and the effects of rain, frost and gravity to

DID YOU KNOW?

Some of the Bantam soldiers were so small that they had to be issued with special short butts for their Lewis guns so they could reach the trigger.

take into account, combined with flooding and instructions to improve sections of trenches, there was always something to be done in the trenches. The problem was when to do it. Work in daylight was bound to attract enemy fire and this therefore was carried out in the dark. Dawn and dusk were judged to be the times when an attack was most likely, as the enemy took advantage of the gloom to get close to his opponent's trench. For this reason, every man in the trench would be ready with fixed bayonet during 'stand to' for half an hour before and after dusk. After it was fully dark some men were kept on sentry duty, standing with head and shoulders above the parapet to ensure that they could see any movement in no-man's-land. The others were divided between those working on the trench or barbed-wire defences, or resting before their turn as sentry or as part of the working parties.

I WAS THERE

At dusk one evening Marshall and I were standing close together talking when a whiz-bang [fast German shell] arrived without warning. There was [a] plonk, some smoke and a shower of dirt which covered us, then all was quiet. We were well and truly shaken. It was clear that the dud missile had actually passed, chest high, between our bodies, which had only been two feet apart. It was a very narrow squeak indeed.

Corporal George Coppard, Machine Gun Corps[13]

DID YOU KNOW?

Both sides used tethered observation balloons. The term 'When the balloon goes up', meaning trouble, comes from the period of trench warfare when an enemy balloon would equate to danger.

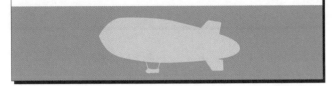

Even though their trench garrison might be quite large, the need to keep some men on sentry duty, others resting and the remainder working meant that the actual number of men on wiring parties or improving the trenches was quite small. This would continue all night, and the long hours of winter darkness gave more time for the work to be carried out. The next morning a routine 'stand to' was followed, in the British Army, by a ration of rum. A small percentage of men were then kept on sentry duty, as low as one in ten, watching through periscopes whilst the rest first breakfasted, washed, shaved and then cleaned their weapons. This was followed by an inspection to ensure that the men's respirators were functioning, their rifles were clean and serviceable, and there was no litter to attract rats. Some tasks, such as sandbag filling

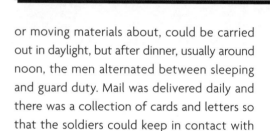

DID YOU KNOW?

The term 'going over the top' was used along with 'hopping the bags' by soldiers in the war.

or moving materials about, could be carried out in daylight, but after dinner, usually around noon, the men alternated between sleeping and guard duty. Mail was delivered daily and there was a collection of cards and letters so that the soldiers could keep in contact with their families at home. Supper was normally before dark, even in winter, and then there was the inevitable 'stand to' before dusk.

Some units went to great lengths to ensure the comfort of the troops and one veteran recalls always receiving hot pea soup on cold nights. This was so regular that he always knew it was midnight when the containers arrived from the kitchens behind the lines. Men were rarely sent to the rear during a tour of duty and carrying parties bringing rations, ammunition or stores were selected from the men who were out of the line, officially resting.

Whatever the time of year, weather conditions or sector of the line, the few days spent in the front line could be boring and uneventful, or marked by shelling, raids or a major attack. Units that had spent long periods in one sector without a casualty would find others to be death traps, where the enemy was more active or alert. When going into the line there was no predicting what was going to happen in the five or so days and nights spent in a muddy ditch called a trench.

OUT OF THE TRENCHES

AS TROOPS SPENT only a minority of their time on active service in the trenches, there was a great deal of time spent behind the lines. Soldiers who had recently arrived from home for their first time in 'France and Flanders', as it was officially called, could expect some time at a training camp. Here the instructors, who wore distinctive yellow armbands and were therefore nicknamed the Canaries, put them through brutal courses to toughen them up for the front.

From here, they were sent in units or batches of reinforcements to join the men already serving at the front. This involved long periods of travel, usually by slow French railways, until a railhead was reached and the men would march. It was rare for men to join a unit that was actually in the line and, as such, they tended to join a unit that was resting. This meant that it was out of the front line but available for working and carrying parties, digging trenches for telephone cables, unloading equipment or, until 1917 when the Labour Corps was established, helping to build roads or new railways.

DID YOU KNOW?

British soldiers liked white rather than red wine and ordered *vin blanc*, but pronounced it 'plonk' – a term still used today for cheap wine.

I WAS THERE

A bathing parade was organised before we returned to the trenches, and we marched to Pont de Nieppe and bathed in the river Lys. Major Watson, the battalion second-in-command was in charge. In the warm summer evening we sported in the water like kids without a care.

Corporal George Coppard, Machine Gun Corps[14]

Men who were with units that were out of the line were eligible for leave, up to ten days each year, and others were selected for specialist training. Sometimes this was because they demonstrated a specific skill, but for many it was to give them a rest from the routine of time spent in the line and then resting. These courses of instruction were run at schools, which were well behind the lines, and courses could last weeks. The schools produced signallers, snipers, gas specialists and even cooks. The result of all these variations of men's service, which was combined with time spent moving units to where they were next required, meant that most soldiers spent no more than 10 per cent of their time in the front line. However, the problem with resting was that men who had come out of the front line carried out all the difficult hard labour, and this was sometimes combined with training for future operations. This kind of training could be very realistic, using live ammunition, and there were fatal accidents. As the war progressed, men had to become familiar with creeping barrages of artillery fire, co-operating with tanks or aircraft, and the details of specific objectives. This kind of training became increasingly common and used scale models or even full-size replicas of the next battlefield.

I WAS THERE

So our walk ended; we passed the looming aerodrome, and line of lorries under the trees along the main road, and the sentry who stood by a glowing brazier at the crossroads. Down in [a] hollow crouched the Camp; a disgusting dinner in the smoky hut and early to bed, was all it could afford us.

Second Lieutenant Siegfried Sassoon, Somme, 1916[15]

For soldiers who were out of the line there was the opportunity to alternate work with football, always enjoyed and encouraged to build team spirit, as well as to buy additional food from the many forces and YMCA canteens, local bars and *estaminets*. Men were given passes that allowed them to be outside camp or away from their unit, although failure to return on time could lead to a charge of 'absent without leave' ('going AWOL'). A longer term away from a unit carried the threat of desertion, which came with a potential death penalty.

As the men were paid in French francs, they could buy beer, wine and chips, normally combined with fried eggs or omelettes. Although the men were well fed, rations lacked variety and chips were a rarity that had been familiar at home when combined with fried fish. In France and Belgium, eggs replaced this and were always welcome. A soldier's evening out could include watching a film; sometimes

DID YOU KNOW?

Compared to British troops, the French had very poor pay, infrequent leave and poor medical treatment. This led to a major mutiny is the spring of 1917.

these were uplifting propaganda, but Charlie Chaplin films were popular escapism. Most divisions had their own group of performers and, as recruitment was so broad, many of these troupes included people who had been professional performers in civilian life. The 56th Division from London had a troupe called the Bow Belles and a performance of variety hall numbers could be enjoyed even though the background might have been distant shelling.

Whatever happened during time out of the line, what was certain was the return to the front line at some point or, more threatening, the promise of the next 'show' or 'stunt', as they were called – this meant battle.

INTO BATTLE OR OVER THE TOP

IF TIME SPENT in the front line was infrequent, then battle was a rarity. Even in a busy year like 1917, when there were four major British offensives, not every unit was involved and, even when they were, it was for a matter of days. However, when the training, increased rations and issues of new equipment indicated that something was being prepared by the top brass it was clear that the men were being 'fattened up', as they put it. Once the battle had been planned and rehearsed, the units that would attack took over their allocated section of line, replacing the men who had previously been there. This usually occurred during the night preceding the battle to ensure that the attackers were rested, fit and ready for attack. Units usually selected a cross section of officers, NCOs and men to be left out of battle. This 10 per cent selection was kept in reserve and would be the basis for a new battalion, should something go wrong on the day of battle.

DID YOU KNOW?

11.8 per cent of British troops died in the war, compared to 13 per cent of French and 16 per cent of Germans.

I WAS THERE

Soon afterwards we were held up by a machine gun firing dead on the trench where it had been damaged, and took refuge in a big shell-hole that had broken into it. Johnson went to fetch Lewis guns and bombers. I could see four or five heads bobbing up and down a little way off so I fired at them and never hit one.

Second Lieutenant Siegfried Sassoon, Somme, 1916[16]

Most battles commenced with a bombardment of the enemy positions, but as the war progressed these became increasingly sophisticated and brief; however, it was rare for the enemy to be completely deceived as to what was planned. One such example occurred at Messines in June 1917. The German defenders were so stunned by the explosion of the gigantic mines under their positions that some of the survivors came forward to surrender to the attackers as they advanced.

The moments before zero hour, the time set for the attack, were always tense. Despite a ration of service rum – never enough to make men drunk but sufficient to warm them on a cold day – the final exchanges among the men about to 'go over the top' or 'hop the bags' would be heartfelt. One term that was often used during the war was, 'See you on the other side', which can be understood to mean in the enemy position or somewhere else.

When the whistle blew and the attack started, the men were frequently not in the trenches but in front of them, in 'jumping-off trenches' dug in no-man's-land, or simply in the cover afforded by the weeds and debris between the trenches. On other occasions, the men went up the assault ladders, as seen in films, but this was rare.

I WAS THERE

Each battalion then extended in four waves to cover about 300 yards of frontage and crawled forward to begin crossing the six to eight hundred yards of No Man's Land … Eight minutes afterwards on the tick of Zero Hour, and following the explosion of the mines under La Boisselle salient, our field gun barrage, till then falling on the first German trench line, now lifted to a further line. Both battalions, rising to their feet, now advanced in quick time through the rank, knee-deep grass, the four waves at one hundred paces interval, to close on the foe with the bayonet.

Brigadier General Jack, Somme, 1916[17]

DID YOU KNOW?

British soldiers referred to Field Marshal Sir Douglas Haig as 'D.H.' or 'The Chief'.

By 1917, the creeping barrage of shells had been developed, and the advance followed this wall of shells as it progressed towards the enemy trenches. On some occasions these shells were highly explosive, detonating when they hit the ground; on other occasions shrapnel shells were used. These were timed to explode in the air, projecting a cloud of fast-moving metallic balls forward and below where they had exploded. This meant that shells were going off in the air above the advancing troops and they had to be careful not to go too fast and walk into their own barrage.

Despite the universal image of British soldiers walking forward in lines with fixed bayonets, the advance was varied to suit the conditions and training of the men involved. Some soldiers ran to get to the objective as quickly as possible, and the artillery barrage was changed to suit this. Others went in leaps and bounds, with some men moving while the others provided them with covering fire. The addition of light machine guns and rifle grenades made this easier, and this tactic was common by early 1917.

In consequence, when the enemy were located or betrayed themselves by opening fire, the attackers could use their machine guns and rifle grenades to pin them down and then close on them with bombs and bayonets.

For a brief period this type of attack tended to develop into a grenade duel along the length of the trench, in which it was difficult for either side to gain an advantage. By mid-war, it was preferred to stay on the surface, getting behind the enemy and, if they were found in dugouts, demolishing the entrances with special charges or incendiaries to prevent defenders appearing behind the first attacking waves. In theory, once the first objective was captured, the men would dig in ready for the enemy counter-attack, while other troops passed through them to continue the advance. Casualties were inevitable, even with a successful attack, and, with tens of thousands of troops advancing, the number of dead and wounded of these massive battles is not surprising.

Co-operation with other units in the advance was vital and, with radios in their infancy, signallers used the telephone with vulnerable cables, flags, lamps, runners and pigeons to get messages to higher command. In some attacks the men had coloured cloths or pieces of tin fastened to the back of their equipment so that the gunners could see how far they had advanced and prevent friendly fire incidents. Tanks would be used to cut the enemy barbed wire and crush strongpoints, and the infantry soon learned to be confident when working with the 'tankies', even if they were prone to breaking down at the wrong moment. While all of this was going on, the pilots of the Royal Flying Corps (or the Royal Air Force from 1 April 1918) were flying contact patrols to monitor the advance, direct artillery and even fly resupply missions of ammunition. The real trench attack was quite different from that seen on the screen.

SICK OR WOUNDED

EVEN IN THE trenches soldiers were never far from a doctor: the regimental medical officer, usually referred to as the MO or 'Doc' by the officers and men of the unit; he would be attached to the unit from the Royal Army Medical Corps. He was the equivalent of a local general practitioner and emergency service rolled into one. He worked in camp, on the march and in the trenches, with the assistance of a medical orderly, a small team of sanitary orderlies and sixteen stretcher bearers who were all selected from the unit and trained by the MO. Every morning the unit had a sick parade and men who suspected themselves of being ill would present themselves at the Regimental Aid Post for diagnosis and treatment. The MO was universally regarded as being harsh in his response to men presenting themselves with a range of real and imaginary ailments. He was aware that lazy soldiers could use his diagnosis to avoid duties. However, there was often a strong bond between the MO and the men, and it is no coincidence that the only man to be awarded two Victoria Crosses during the First World War was a regimental medical officer.

I WAS THERE

During the day one of the men of the 5th Scottish Rifles on our right noticed a wounded man of ours lying out in front who was trying to crawl back to the trench. He jumped over the parapet and ran towards him and under heavy fire of rifle-bullets safely brought him back to his trench. He was awarded the Victoria Cross.

Private Frank Richards, Somme[11]

DID YOU KNOW?
The double Victoria Crosses, both awarded in the war, went to Doctor Noel Chavasse. Sadly, his last award was posthumous.

In the trenches, the MO continued to care for the men, doing his rounds to inspect mess tins and toilets, rations and the men's feet. In wet conditions, trench foot could destroy circulation in men's feet and in the worst untreated cases this could lead to loss of toes or worse. Many MOs took to ensuring that the rations sent to the trenches were hot and of good quality, and that the men had the opportunity to receive dry socks and, if possible, 'whale oil', which was rubbed into the feet to provide a waterproof layer. Of course, every day there would also be men on sick parade who would have to be treated or sent to the rear for better treatment down the chain of evacuation through a relay of aid posts and clearing stations.

In action this was also the situation for casualties. With only one MO, he could rarely leave his post and attend to a wounded man in the trenches. Every man had a field dressing in a pocket sewn into his uniform and the MO trained everyone how to apply

DID YOU KNOW?

The war led to the routine use of motor ambulances, blood transfusion, better plastic surgery and the extensive use of X-ray equipment, which are all features of modern hospitals.

this to his own or his mate's wounds. If he could walk, a wounded man then made his way to the Regimental Aid Post. If not, the stretcher bearers would recover the wounded man, having dressed his wounds if this was necessary. At the Regimental Aid Post, the MO would assess the wounded man's situation to see if he was fit to travel by stretcher back to the Advanced Dressing Station behind the lines. The MO would make sure that blood loss was controlled, that the man did not have a fractured limb, that his pain level was controlled by morphine, that he had an anti-tetanus injection and that he was not going into shock. The Regimental Aid Post provided men with warm blankets, tea, cigarettes and sometimes a biscuit, all in an effort to prevent them from becoming chilled and to replace lost fluids. In the days before the regular use of blood for transfusion, a mug of hot, sweet tea

I WAS THERE

The next thing I knew was when I came to and found myself remembering a tremendous blow in the throat and right shoulder and feeling speechless and paralysed. Men were moving to and fro above me. Then there was a wild yell — 'They're coming back' and I was alone.

Second Lieutenant Siegfried Sassoon, Somme, 1916[13]

was regarded as doing wonders for wounded men. Only once all these checks had been made would a wounded man be judged fit to travel to the rear. If not, he would be made as comfortable as possible in the cramped trenches and left until later, if he survived.

The Regimental Aid Post was not a miniature hospital and can be regarded as fulfilling the function of an ambulance today. It provided basic, quick treatment to ensure that patients would survive before they were sent to the rear through a succession of increasingly sophisticated medical facilities. Although, sadly, many soldiers died on the battlefield and others during evacuation, 70 per cent of the wounded returned to the front line. To get some idea of the scale of injuries, it must be realised that more doses of anti-tetanus serum were administered than there were men in the entire British Army between 1914 and 1918. Unfortunately, in a world before antibiotics, many men died of wounds from which they would have later recovered.

FOOD IN THE TRENCHES

THE RATIONS SOLDIERS were provided with in the trenches has received little attention beyond Private Balderick's offer of 'Rat O Van' to Captain Edmund Blackadder in the television series *Blackadder Goes Forth*. There is a general belief that food in the trenches was always cold, tasteless or simply absent. The reality is rather different. When soldiers were in training or behind the lines they were entitled to a ration of 1lb of fresh or frozen meat plus bacon, 1lb of bread, fresh vegetables, tea, sugar, milk, pickles and cheese. In the trenches, all the fresh ingredients were replaced with tinned meat, dried vegetables and biscuits. The idea was that the soldier would receive the same number of calories but in a manner that could be dealt with under trench conditions. For emergency use, every soldier carried 'iron rations' of tea, biscuit and tinned meat, and these were only to be used on the orders of an officer when no other food was available.

DID YOU KNOW?

British soldiers referred to Maconochie meat and vegetable stew as 'dog vomit', while French soldiers called bully beef *singe* or monkey.

I WAS THERE

*The following day we were without food and
water and during the night some of us were
out searching the dead to see if they had been
carrying any with them. I was lucky enough to
discover a half-loaf of bread, some biscuits and
two bottles of water, which I would not have sold
for a thousand pounds.*

Private Frank Richards, Arras, 1917[20]

DID YOU KNOW?
Modern archaeology has found plenty of evidence of sauces and pickles in the trenches, together with full tins of food that were clearly dumped by soldiers who were sick of the taste or weight of tins of beans or bully beef.

Rations were sent up from behind the lines on a daily basis in two forms. The first was the meals, soups and occasionally hot drinks that were prepared by the company cooks. Every company, of 200 men, had a wheeled cooker that could be pulled behind a horse on the march. This system was helped by the development of 'hay boxes'. These were initially ration crates in which a dixie, or lidded food container, was transported to the trenches surrounded by hay. This insulation not only ensured that the food remained hot, but it actually helped it continue to cook. Later, special metal containers that could be worn like a backpack were developed.

It is not difficult to appreciate what an advantage hot meals would be for men in a cold, wet trench. It was clearly impossible for a limited number of cooks to provide constant hot meals for hundreds of men when smoke could betray their position and lead to shelling;

as well, the trenches covered such a wide area. In consequence, most soldiers had to rely on rations prepared behind the lines by the cooks and quartermasters, and delivered in the ever-useful sandbag. A section of men consisted of around eight to ten individuals and it was possible to calculate the 'ration strength' of any unit on a daily basis. With this information, the appropriate rations were requested and the Army Service Corps delivered these to the unit every day. As a battalion could be a thousand men strong, this involved a great deal of transport and the bulk of the rations is difficult to imagine.

However, once delivered the rations were divided up into lots, each destined for one section of men. Loose tea and sugar went either into paper bags or, more commonly, the corner of the sandbag that was tied off in a knot. The biscuits, which were really preserved flour, could be tipped into the bag together with tinned corned beef – 'bully beef' to the troops – Maconochie meat and vegetable (tinned stew) rations, which were loved by some and hated by others. In addition, tinned condensed milk, cheese, bacon, pickles and tinned jam all joined the heavy and bulky goods. The bag was then sent forward at night by carrying parties so that they were ready for the start of each day.

I WAS THERE

Sharing rations for a small unit was a bit of a lottery, especially where tins of jam, bully beef, pork and beans, butter and so on were concerned … wrapping loose rations such as tea, cheese and meat was not considered necessary, all being tipped into a sandbag, a ghastly mix-up resulting.

Corporal George Coppard, Machine Gun Corps[21]

DID YOU KNOW?

A 'Tommy cooker' was a small tin containing solid fuel that could be used to cook food or warm water for tea.

Meals where therefore much the same each day and boredom could only be offset by soldiers buying their own pickles and sauces to 'liven up' meals. Breakfast was usually fried bacon and tea, perhaps with cheese. The noonday meal was either bully beef as it was or a stew cooked in the soldier's mess tin together with dried vegetables, a stock cube and some biscuit thickening. Supper or tea was the last meal of the day and usually consisted of whatever was left over, with jam, cheese and tea being common. Much depended upon the skill of the soldier, and men often worked as 'mess mates', with one responsible for cooking whilst the other made tea.

Tea was the most common drink and this was always very sweet and strong; there is no doubt that this drink made a massive contribution to the war effort – perhaps second only to tobacco. The men received cigarettes or pipe tobacco and, like food, these could be bought, together with chocolate and 'Tommy cookers' from the canteens behind the lines. Few soldiers went into the trenches, if they had the money, without their pack and pockets being stuffed with extras, just in case. It can be easily imagined that a later wagon or a shell that hit a ration party would leave men hungry and angry as they waited for the vital rations that would see them through the next twenty-four hours.

THE TRENCHES TODAY

AT THE END of the war, when the armies stopped fighting as agreed in the Armistice of 11 November 1918, large areas of France and Belgium were left devastated and crisscrossed by trenches. However, every field, wood, lane and track belonged to a farmer or landowner. Many had fled to Britain or areas of France, well away from the fighting. The end of the war meant that these owners and tenants could return to pick up what was left of their pre-war lives. For the majority this was farming, and resuming cultivation meant clearing away the debris of war, burying the dead and filling in the trenches. Although this process took years to complete, the result was that trenches were preserved only in a few places.

Around Hill 60 at Ypres, the damage caused by mining and counter-mining meant that this area was grazed by sheep but could never be farmed. To the east of Ypres, and close to Sanctuary Wood just off the Menin Road, a post-war farmer turned the trenches he found in 1919 into a tourist attraction and they are still visited by thousands of people each year. It is difficult to be certain whether these are real trenches or just follow the same line as the originals, but hordes of students stomp through the mud they contain, to the obvious discomfort of generations of coach drivers.

At Beaumont Hamel on the Somme, the Newfoundland people were granted an area of battlefield as a permanent memorial to the casualties of that small colony in the First World War. Now the Newfoundland Memorial, the lines of trenches it contains are preserved under turf close cropped by sheep, a vestige of their former size and shape. Further north, the Canadian people received the site of their great victory of 1917 when they were granted Vimy Ridge by a grateful French Government. Here the craters were left much as they were, but both Allied and German trenches were reconstructed with concrete-filled sandbags and they remain in this condition today.

More recently, archaeology has meant that some stretches of trenches have been excavated in the interest of research. Much as after the war, most of these lines of trenches have been back-filled so that farming can resume. Exceptions include the communication trenches in Auchonvillers and Thiepval Wood on the Somme, and in the industrial estate near Boezinge at Ypres. However well these trenches are preserved, it takes imagination and information to repopulate them with their garrisons of First World War soldiers. I hope that this book helps you to understand trench warfare and trench life, even if you never step foot into the clay of Flanders or upon the chalk of the Somme.

NOTES

1   Gilby, Thomas, *Britain at Arms* (Eyre & Spottiswoode, 1953), p. 92.
2   Ibid., p. 182.
3   General Staff, *Report on Foreign Manoeuvres in 1912* (War Office, 1912).
4   Bloem, Walter, *The Advance from Mons 1914* (Helion & Co., 2004), p. 41.
5   Richards, Frank, *Old Soldiers Never Die* (Naval & Military Press, 2001), p. 35.
6   Coleman, Frederick, *From Mons to Ypres with French: A Personal Narrative* (Sampson Law, Morton & Co. Ltd, 1916).
7   Richards, op. cit., p. 67.
8   Terraine, John, *General Jack's Diary* (Cassell & Co., 2000), p. 85.
9   Ibid., p. 108.
10 Junger, Ernst, *The Storm of Steel* (Zimmermann & Zimmermann, 1985), p. 97.
11 Coppard, George, *With a Machine Gun to Cambrai* (Cassell & Co., 1980).
12 Richards, op. cit., p. 297.
13 Coppard, op. cit., p. 93.
14 Ibid., p. 24.
15 Sassoon, Siegfried, *Memoirs of an Infantry Officer* (Faber & Faber, 1965), p. 70.
16 Ibid., p. 59.
17 Terraine, op. cit., p. 144.
18 Richards, op. cit., battle 166.
19 Sassoon, op. cit., p. 167.

20 Richards, op. cit., p. 230.
21 Coppard, op. cit., p. 43.

SELECT BIBLIOGRAPHY

Bloem, Walter, *The Advance from Mons 1914* (Helion & Co., 2004)

Bull, Stephen, *Trench Warfare* (PRC Publishing, 2003)

Coombs, Rose E.B., *Before Endeavours Fade* (After The Battle, 2006)

Coppard, George, *With a Machine Gun to Cambrai* (Cassell & Co., 1980)

Gilby, Thomas, *Britain at Arms* (Eyre & Spottiswoode, 1953)

Holt, Tonie & Volmie, *Major and Mrs Holt's Battlefield Guide: The Western Front* (Pen & Sword, 2004)

Junger, Ernst, *The Storm of Steel* (Zimmermann & Zimmermann, 1985)

Richards, Frank, *Old Soldiers Never Die* (Naval & Military Press, 2001)

Robertshaw, Andrew, *24hr Trench* (The History Press, 2012)

Robertshaw, Andrew, *Feeding Tommy: Battlefield Recipes from the First World War* (The History Press, 2013)

Sassoon, Siegfried, *Memoirs of an Infantry Officer* (Faber & Faber, 1965)

Terraine, John, *General Jack's Diary* (Cassell & Co., 2000)

Excellent reproduction trench maps are available from:

G.H. Smith & Son
Easingwold
York
YO6 3AB
www.ghsmithbookshop.com

Discover more books in this series ...

5 MINUTE HISTORY

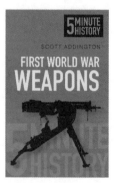
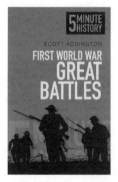
Visit our website and discover thousands
of other History Press books.

www.thehistorypress.co.uk

The History Press